THIS little LIGHT OF MINE

The Bible Promise Book®

BARBOUR BOOKS
An Imprint of Barbour Publishing, Inc.

Our mission is to inspire the world with the life-changing message of the Bible.

Member of the
Evangelical Christian
Publishers Association

*U*sing a childlike approach to God's promises and prayer, this book is a simple and fun way to help your little one shine their light while learning about serving God. With kid-friendly scriptures that highlight each topic, this Bible Promise book is the perfect way to fill your child's heart with the truth of God's Word while teaching your child how to live for Him every day!

DEAR GOD,
THANK YOU FOR
YOUR PROMISES.
AMEN.

✦ CONTENTS ✦

anger

I NEED GOD'S HELP
WHEN I'M MAD.
HE ALWAYS
MAKES ME FEEL BETTER.

Now is the time to get rid of anger.

COLOSSIANS 3:8 NLT

A GENTLE ANSWER TURNS AWAY ANGER,
BUT A SHARP WORD CAUSES ANGER.

PROVERBS 15:1

Hot tempers start fights;
a calm, cool spirit keeps the peace.

PROVERBS 15:18 MSG

If you are angry, do not let it become sin.
Get over your anger before the day is finished.

EPHESIANS 4:26

Smart people know how
to hold their tongue.

PROVERBS 19:11 MSG

Do not be quick in spirit to be angry.
For anger is in the heart of fools.

ECCLESIASTES 7:9

Don't hang out with angry people;
don't keep company with hotheads.
Bad temper is contagious—
don't get infected.

PROVERBS 22:24–25 MSG

HE WHO IS SLOW TO GET ANGRY HAS GREAT UNDERSTANDING.

PROVERBS 14:29

Stop being angry.
Turn away from fighting.
Do not trouble yourself.
It leads only to wrong-doing.

PSALM 37:8

GOD IS ALL MERCY AND GRACE— NOT QUICK TO ANGER, IS RICH IN LOVE.

PSALM 145:8 MSG

Everyone should listen much and speak little.
He should be slow to become angry.

JAMES 1:19

Work at getting along with
each other and with God.

HEBREWS 12:14 MSG

Don't insist on getting even;
that's not for you to do.
"I'll do the judging," says God.
"I'll take care of it."

ROMANS 12:19 MSG

WISE MEN TURN AWAY ANGER.

PROVERBS 29:8

Do all things without arguing
and talking about how you wish you
did not have to do them. . . .
You are to shine as lights among
the sinful people of this world.

PHILIPPIANS 2:14–15

A man who hurts people tempts
his neighbor to do the same,
and leads him in a way
that is not good.
PROVERBS 16:29

HE WHO IS SLOW TO ANGER IS BETTER THAN THE POWERFUL.

PROVERBS 16:32

A dry piece of food with peace
and quiet is better than a house
full of food with fighting.
PROVERBS 17:1

Don't hit back.
ROMANS 12:17 MSG

dear God,
when i get mad,
please help me
to be nice.

amen.

courage

WITH GOD'S HELP,
I CAN DO ANYTHING!

I can do all things because
Christ gives me the strength.

PHILIPPIANS 4:13

BY NOT GIVING UP, GOD'S WORD
GIVES US STRENGTH AND HOPE.

ROMANS 15:4

"Peace I leave with you.
My peace I give to you.
I do not give peace to you
as the world gives.
Do not let your hearts
be troubled or afraid."

JOHN 14:27

YOU ARE MY WONDERFUL GOD WHO GIVES ME COURAGE.

PSALM 3:3 ICB

Let us keep looking to Jesus.
Our faith comes from
Him and He is the One
Who makes it perfect.

HEBREWS 12:2

"Come to Me, all of you who
work and have heavy loads.
I will give you rest."

MATTHEW 11:28

May [God] give your hearts
comfort and strength to say
and do every good thing.

2 Thessalonians 2:17

GOD HAS POWER OVER ALL THINGS FOREVER.

1 Peter 5:11

I am happy to be weak and have
troubles so I can have Christ's power
in me. I receive joy when I am weak.
I receive joy when people talk against
me and make it hard for me and try
to hurt me and make trouble for me.
I receive joy when all these things
come to me because of Christ.
For when I am weak,
then I am strong.

2 Corinthians 12:9–10

We will receive [God's]
loving-kindness and have
His loving-favor to help
us whenever we need it.

HEBREWS 4:16

GOD. . .GIVES YOU STRENGTH.

ROMANS 15:5

If we are sure [God]
hears us when we ask,
we can be sure He will give
us what we ask for.

1 JOHN 5:15

"IN THE WORLD YOU WILL HAVE
MUCH TROUBLE. BUT TAKE HOPE!
I HAVE POWER OVER THE WORLD!"

JOHN 16:33

There is only one God.
He is the Father.
All things are from Him.
He made us for Himself.
There is one Lord.
He is Jesus Christ.
He made all things.
He keeps us alive.

1 CORINTHIANS 8:6

dear God,
thank you for
helping me be brave
when i have to do things
that aren't easy.
amen.

faith

I BELIEVE IN MY HEART
THAT GOD WILL DO WHAT
HE SAYS. THAT'S FAITH!

You must have faith as you
ask [God]. You must not doubt.
Anyone who doubts is like a
wave which is pushed around by the sea.

JAMES 1:6

YOU ARE ALL CHILDREN OF GOD THROUGH FAITH IN CHRIST JESUS.

GALATIANS 3:26 NLT

You have never seen [God] but you love Him.
You cannot see Him now but
you are putting your trust in Him.
And you have joy so great that
words cannot tell about it.

1 PETER 1:8

Now faith is being sure we will get what we hope for. It is being sure of what we cannot see.

HEBREWS 11:1

"ANYTHING IS POSSIBLE IF A PERSON BELIEVES."

MARK 9:23 NLT

If we have no faith, [God] will still be faithful for He cannot go against what He is.

2 TIMOTHY 2:13

If you say with your mouth that Jesus is Lord, and believe in your heart that God raised Him from the dead, you will be saved from the punishment of sin.

ROMANS 10:9

Jesus said to him, "Thomas, because you have seen Me, you believe. Those are happy who have never seen Me and yet believe!"

JOHN 20:29

I will give thanks to the Lord with all my heart. I will tell of all the great things You have done.

PSALM 9:1

Let us come near to God with a true heart full of faith. Our hearts must be made clean from guilty feelings and our bodies washed with pure water.

HEBREWS 10:22

GET YOUR STRENGTH FROM [JESUS].

COLOSSIANS 2:7

God makes all things work together for
the good of those who love Him.

ROMANS 8:28

We can trust God that He will do what He promised.

HEBREWS 10:23

LOVE THE LORD, ALL YOU WHO BELONG TO
HIM! THE LORD KEEPS THE FAITHFUL SAFE.

PSALM 31:23

"[God] keeps His promise and shows His
loving-kindness to those who love Him."

DEUTERONOMY 7:9

BE HAPPY IN THE LORD. AND HE WILL GIVE
YOU THE DESIRES OF YOUR HEART.

PSALM 37:4

---

*"I have loved you just as My Father
has loved Me. Stay in My love."*

JOHN 15:9

---

*"And you must love the Lord your God with
all your heart and with all your soul
and with all your strength."*

DEUTERONOMY 6:5

---

*You have turned my crying into dancing.
You have. . .dressed me with joy.*

PSALM 30:11

dear God,
i have faith in
your promises. i know if you
say it, you'll do it!
amen.

fear

I DON'T EVER NEED TO
BE AFRAID, BECAUSE GOD
PROMISES TO PROTECT ME
AND LOVE ME—ALWAYS!

When I am afraid,
I will trust in [God].

PSALM 56:3

I WILL NOT BE AFRAID BECAUSE THE LORD IS WITH ME.

PSALM 118:6 ICB

Who can keep us away from the love of Christ?
Can trouble or problems? . . . [Nothing can]
keep us away from the love of God which
is ours through Christ Jesus our Lord.

ROMANS 8:35, 39

"DO NOT BE AFRAID! BE STRONG,
AND SEE HOW THE LORD
WILL SAVE YOU TODAY."

Exodus 14:13

---

*I will not be afraid of anything,
because [God is] with me.*

Psalm 23:4

---

*"See, God saves me. I will trust and not be afraid.
For the Lord God is my strength and song."*

Isaiah 12:2

---

*Do not be afraid. . . . Have joy and be glad,
for the Lord has done great things.*

Joel 2:21

"Do not fear, for I am with you.
Do not be afraid, for I am your God."

ISAIAH 41:10

THOSE WHO DO RIGHT DO NOT HAVE TO BE AFRAID.

ROMANS 13:3

You will not be afraid when you lie down.
When you lie down, your sleep will be sweet.

PROVERBS 3:24

"Do not be afraid. I am the
First and the Last."

REVELATION 1:17

"Be strong and have strength of heart! Do not be afraid or lose faith. For the Lord your God is with you anywhere you go."

JOSHUA 1:9

"Do not be afraid. You are more important than many small birds."

MATTHEW 10:31

"I AM WITH YOU TO TAKE YOU OUT OF TROUBLE," SAYS THE LORD.

JEREMIAH 1:8

"Do not be afraid, just believe."

MARK 5:36

DO NOT BE AFRAID OF THOSE WHO HATE YOU.

PHILIPPIANS 1:28

"The Lord is my Helper.
I am not afraid of anything
man can do to me."

HEBREWS 13:6

"God knows how many hairs you have
on your head. Do not be afraid."

LUKE 12:7

[God said,] "Do not be afraid. . . .
You are Mine!"

ISAIAH 43:1

dear God,
thank you for protecting
me. because you are always
with me, i don't ever have to
be afraid of anything!
amen.

forgiveness

WHEN SOMEONE HURTS
MY FEELINGS AND I FORGIVE
THEM, GOD IS PROUD OF ME.
I ALWAYS WANT TO MAKE
GOD HAPPY.

"THE FORGIVENESS YOU GIVE TO
OTHERS WILL BE GIVEN TO YOU."

MATTHEW 7:2 ICB

You must be kind to each other.
Think of the other person.
Forgive other people just
as God forgave you.

EPHESIANS 4:32

Forgive anyone who offends you.
Remember, the Lord forgave you,
so you must forgive others.

COLOSSIANS 3:13 NLT

*"Do not fight with the man
who wants to fight."*

Matthew 5:39

---

*When someone does something bad to you,
do not do the same thing to him. When someone
talks about you, do not talk about him. Instead,
pray that good will come to him. You were called to
do this so you might receive good things from God.*

1 Peter 3:9

"IF ONE SINNER IS SORRY FOR HIS SINS AND TURNS FROM THEM, THE ANGELS ARE VERY HAPPY."

Luke 15:10

"IF YOU FORGIVE PEOPLE THEIR SINS,
YOUR FATHER IN HEAVEN WILL
FORGIVE YOUR SINS ALSO."

MATTHEW 6:14

---

*Peter came to Jesus and said, "Lord, how many
times may my brother sin against me and I forgive
him, up to seven times?" Jesus said to him, "I tell
you, not seven times but seventy times seven!"*

MATTHEW 18:21–22

---

*"Forgive other people and other
people will forgive you."*

LUKE 6:37

FOR YOU ARE GOOD AND READY TO FORGIVE,
O LORD. YOU ARE RICH IN LOVING-KINDNESS
TO ALL WHO CALL TO YOU.

PSALM 86:5

The Lord does not want any person to be punished
forever. He wants all people to be sorry
for their sins and turn from them.

2 PETER 3:9

It will not go well for the man who hides his
sins, but he who tells his sins and turns
from them will be given loving-pity.

PROVERBS 28:13

*"But you must be sorry for your
sins and turn from them.
You must turn to God and
have your sins taken away.
Then many times your soul
will receive new strength
from the Lord."*

ACTS 3:19

---

*"You must be sorry for this sin
of yours and turn from it. Pray
to the Lord that He will forgive."*

ACTS 8:22

**"ANYONE WHO BELIEVES IN GOD'S
SON HAS ETERNAL LIFE."**

JOHN 3:36 NLT

Anyone who belongs to Christ has become a new person. The old life is gone; a new life has begun!

2 Corinthians 5:17 NLT

HE WASHED AWAY OUR SINS, GIVING US A NEW BIRTH AND NEW LIFE THROUGH THE HOLY SPIRIT.

Titus 3:5 NLT

BECOME FRIENDS WITH GOD; HE'S ALREADY A
FRIEND WITH YOU. HOW? YOU ASK. IN CHRIST.
GOD PUT THE WRONG ON HIM WHO NEVER
DID ANYTHING WRONG, SO WE COULD
BE PUT RIGHT WITH GOD.

2 CORINTHIANS 5:20–21 MSG

---

*[God] wants all people to be saved from the
punishment of sin. He wants them to
come to know the truth.*

1 TIMOTHY 2:4

dear God,
when someone hurts my
feelings, i need your help to
forgive them. and when i
make a mistake, thank you
for forgiving me!
amen.

friendship

GOD WANTS ME TO BE
A GOOD FRIEND. HIS WORD
SHOWS ME HOW.

A FRIEND LOVES AT ALL TIMES.

PROVERBS 17:17

"Do for other people what you would like to have them do for you."

LUKE 6:31

Think of other people as more important than yourself.

PHILIPPIANS 2:3

A man who has friends must be a friend.

PROVERBS 18:24

Love never comes to an end.

1 CORINTHIANS 13:8

Let us love each other,
because love comes from God.

1 JOHN 4:7

HELP EACH OTHER IN TROUBLES
AND PROBLEMS.

GALATIANS 6:2

"You are to love each other. You must love
each other as I have loved you."

JOHN 13:34

Do not leave your own friend. . .alone.

PROVERBS 27:10

*"Do to others whatever you would
like them to do to you."*

MATTHEW 7:12 NLT

---

*"No one can have greater love than to
give his life for his friends."*

JOHN 15:13

---

*If either of them falls down,
one can help the other up.*

ECCLESIASTES 4:10 NIV

WE SHOULD DO GOOD TO EVERYONE.

GALATIANS 6:10

dear God,
thank you for my friends.
help me to always treat
them just the way
i want to be treated.

amen.

happiness

MY HEART IS ALWAYS
HAPPY WHEN I PUT
MY TRUST IN GOD.

*"Those who hear the Word of God
and obey it are happy."*

LUKE 11:28

BE HAPPY IN THE LORD.

PSALM 37:4

---

*If someone has the gift of showing kindness to
others, he should be happy as he does it.*

ROMANS 12:8

Happy is the man who cares for the poor.

PSALM 41:1

A glad heart makes a happy face.

PROVERBS 15:13

I AM MADE HAPPY BY [GOD'S] WORD.

PSALM 119:162

---

*"Those who are hungry and thirsty to
be right with God are happy."*

MATTHEW 5:6

Love is happy with the truth.

1 CORINTHIANS 13:6

Happy is the person who trusts the Lord.

PSALM 40:4 ICB

"My heart is happy in the Lord."

1 SAMUEL 2:1

"Those who make peace are happy,
because they will be called the sons of God."

MATTHEW 5:9

O taste and see that the Lord is good.
How happy is the man who trusts in Him!

PSALM 34:8

We are happy for the hope we have of sharing
the shining-greatness of God.

ROMANS 5:2

FOR YOU WILL MAKE THOSE HAPPY
WHO DO WHAT IS RIGHT, O LORD.

PSALM 5:12

"And my spirit is happy in God."

"Those who show loving-kindness are happy, because they will have loving-kindness shown to them."

MATTHEW 5:7

"WE ARE MORE HAPPY WHEN WE GIVE THAN WHEN WE RECEIVE."

ACTS 20:35

My soul will be happy in the Lord. It will be full of joy because He saves.

PSALM 35:9

"THOSE WHO HAVE A PURE HEART ARE HAPPY,
BECAUSE THEY WILL SEE GOD."

MATTHEW 5:8

Be happy in the Lord your God.

JOEL 2:23

Happy is the nation whose God is the Lord.
Happy are the people He has
chosen for His own.

PSALM 33:12

dear God,
i know i can trust you
with all my heart.
that makes me happy!
amen.

heaven

SOMEDAY I WILL LIVE
FOREVER WITH
GOD IN HEAVEN.

"THERE IS MORE THAN ENOUGH ROOM IN MY
FATHER'S HOME. IF THIS WERE NOT SO, WOULD
I HAVE TOLD YOU THAT I AM GOING TO PREPARE
A PLACE FOR YOU? WHEN EVERYTHING IS READY,
I WILL COME AND GET YOU, SO THAT YOU WILL
ALWAYS BE WITH ME WHERE I AM."

JOHN 14:2–3 NLT

---

*God is keeping careful watch over us and the
future. The Day is coming when you'll have
it all—life healed and whole.*

1 PETER 1:5 MSG

---

*There is a crown which comes from being right
with God. The Lord, the One Who will judge,
will give it to me on that great
day when He comes again.*

2 TIMOTHY 4:8

"My sheep hear My voice and I know them.
They follow Me. I give them life that lasts
forever. They will never be punished.
No one is able to take them out of My hand."

John 10:27–28

GOD'S FREE GIFT IS LIFE THAT LASTS FOREVER. IT IS GIVEN TO US BY OUR LORD JESUS CHRIST.

Romans 6:23

Our body is like a house we live in here on earth.
When it is destroyed, we know that God has
another body for us in heaven. The new one
will not be made by human hands as a
house is made. This body will last forever.

2 Corinthians 5:1

Our human bodies made from dust must be changed into a body that cannot be destroyed. Our human bodies that can die must be changed into bodies that will never die.

1 CORINTHIANS 15:53

"God will take away all tears from their eyes."

REVELATION 7:17

WE ARE LOOKING FOR WHAT GOD HAS PROMISED, WHICH ARE NEW HEAVENS AND A NEW EARTH. ONLY WHAT IS RIGHT AND GOOD WILL BE THERE.

2 PETER 3:13

IF A MAN DOES THINGS TO PLEASE HIS SINFUL
OLD SELF, HIS SOUL WILL BE LOST. IF A MAN
DOES THINGS TO PLEASE THE HOLY SPIRIT,
HE WILL HAVE LIFE THAT LASTS FOREVER.

GALATIANS 6:8

---

*Jesus said. . . , "I am the One Who raises the dead
and gives them life. Anyone who puts his trust in
Me will live again, even if he dies. Anyone who
lives and has put his trust in Me
will never die. Do you believe this?"*

JOHN 11:25–26

---

*He will give eternal life to those who keep
on doing good, seeking after the glory
and honor and immortality that God offers.*

ROMANS 2:7 NLT

The Holy Spirit raised Jesus from the dead.
If the same Holy Spirit lives in you, He will give
life to your bodies in the same way.

ROMANS 8:11

THERE WILL BE NO NIGHT [IN HEAVEN]. THERE WILL BE NO NEED FOR A LIGHT OR FOR THE SUN. BECAUSE THE LORD GOD WILL BE THEIR LIGHT.

REVELATION 22:5

"Anyone who hears My Word and puts his trust
in Him Who sent Me has life that lasts forever.
He will not be guilty. He has already
passed from death into life."

JOHN 5:24

CHRIST HAS GONE TO HEAVEN
AND IS ON THE RIGHT SIDE OF GOD.
ANGELS AND POWERS OF HEAVEN
ARE OBEYING HIM.

1 PETER 3:22

The world and all its desires will pass away.
But the man who obeys God and
does what He wants done
will live forever.

1 JOHN 2:17

*We will receive the great things that we have
been promised. They are being kept safe
in heaven for us. They are pure and
will not pass away. They will
never be lost.*

1 PETER 1:4

"WHY DO YOU STAND LOOKING UP INTO
HEAVEN? THIS SAME JESUS WHO WAS
TAKEN FROM YOU INTO HEAVEN WILL
RETURN IN THE SAME WAY YOU
SAW HIM GO UP INTO HEAVEN."

ACTS 1:11

dear God,
thank you for making
a home for me in heaven!
amen.

honesty

GOD WANTS ME TO TELL THE TRUTH—ALWAYS. HE NEVER WANTS ME TO TELL A LIE.

The LORD detests the use of dishonest scales,
but he delights in accurate weights.

PROVERBS 11:1 NLT

WE WANT TO DO THE RIGHT THING. WE WANT GOD AND MEN TO KNOW WE ARE HONEST.

2 CORINTHIANS 8:21

Stand firm then, with the belt of truth
buckled around your waist.

EPHESIANS 6:14 NIV

The Lord gives favor and honor. He holds back
nothing good from those who walk in
the way that is right.

PSALM 84:11

The LORD. . .delights in people
who are trustworthy.

PROVERBS 12:22 NIV

A little earned in a right way is better than
much earned in a wrong way.

PROVERBS 16:8

DEAR CHILDREN, LET US NOT LOVE WITH WORDS OR SPEECH BUT WITH ACTIONS AND IN TRUTH.

1 JOHN 3:18 NIV

GOOD THINGS WILL BE GIVEN TO THOSE WHO ARE RIGHT WITH GOD.

PROVERBS 13:21

The Lord is near to all who call on Him,
to all who call on Him in truth.

PSALM 145:18

Love does not delight in evil
but rejoices with the truth.

1 CORINTHIANS 13:6 NIV

Speak the truth to each other.

ZECHARIAH 8:16 NIV

I HAVE NO GREATER JOY THAN TO HEAR THAT MY CHILDREN ARE WALKING IN THE TRUTH.

3 JOHN 1:4 NIV

"Do not lie."

LEVITICUS 19:11 NIV

For You will make those happy
who do what is right, O Lord.

PSALM 5:12

DO NOT DO WRONG TO ONE ANOTHER.

LEVITICUS 25:17

dear God,
i will be honest
because i know it
makes you happy!
amen.

hope

MY HOPE COMES FROM
GOD AND HIS PROMISES TO
ME. HE HAS ONLY THE BEST
THINGS PLANNED FOR ME.

*Hope means we are waiting for
something we do not have.*

ROMANS 8:24

I will put my hope in God!

PSALM 42:11 NLT

DEAR FRIENDS, WE ARE ALREADY GOD'S CHILDREN.

1 JOHN 3:2 NLT

---

*We know that troubles help us learn not
to give up. When we have learned not to
give up, it shows we have stood the test.
When we have stood the test,
it gives us hope.*

ROMANS 5:3–4

The hope of the righteous will be gladness.

PROVERBS 10:28 NKJV

---

*Because Jesus was raised from the dead,
we've been given a brand-new life and have
everything to live for, including a future in heaven.*

1 PETER 1:3 MSG

"GOOD WILL COME TO THE MAN WHO TRUSTS
IN THE LORD, AND WHOSE HOPE IS
IN THE LORD."

JEREMIAH 17:7

*We believe that Jesus died and then came to life
again. Because we believe this, we know that God
will bring to life again all those who belong to Jesus.*

1 THESSALONIANS 4:14

YOU ARE MY HIDING PLACE. . . .
I PUT MY HOPE IN YOUR WORD.

PSALM 119:114

---

*It's a good thing to quietly hope,
quietly hope for help from GOD.*

LAMENTATIONS 3:26 MSG

I have put my hope in [God's] Word.

PSALM 119:81

This truth also gives hope of life that lasts forever. God promised this before the world began. He cannot lie.

WE ARE OF GOD'S HOUSE IF WE KEEP OUR TRUST IN THE LORD UNTIL THE END. THIS IS OUR HOPE.

We who have turned to [God] can have great comfort knowing that He will do what He has promised. This hope is a safe anchor for our souls. It will never move.

Our hope comes from God. May He fill you with
joy and peace because of your trust in Him.
May your hope grow stronger by
the power of the Holy Spirit.

ROMANS 15:13

I hope for Your saving power,
O Lord, and I follow Your Word.

PSALM 119:166

WE SPEAK WITHOUT FEAR BECAUSE
OUR TRUST IS IN CHRIST.

2 CORINTHIANS 3:12

I pray that you will know about the hope given by God's call. I pray that you will see how great the things are that He has promised to those who belong to Him.

EPHESIANS 1:18

I hope very much that I will have no reason to be ashamed. I hope to honor Christ with my body. . . . I want to honor Him without fear, now and always.

PHILIPPIANS 1:20

WHY AM I DISCOURAGED? WHY IS MY HEART SO SAD? I WILL PUT MY HOPE IN GOD! I WILL PRAISE HIM AGAIN—MY SAVIOR AND MY GOD!

PSALM 42:11 NLT

WE THANK GOD FOR THE HOPE THAT IS BEING KEPT FOR YOU IN HEAVEN. YOU FIRST HEARD ABOUT THIS HOPE THROUGH THE GOOD NEWS WHICH IS THE WORD OF TRUTH.

COLOSSIANS 1:5

Now faith is being sure we will get what we hope for. It is being sure of what we cannot see.

HEBREWS 11:1

dear God,
my hope is in you
and your promises.
thank you for being
so good to me!
amen.

hurts

GOD WILL ALWAYS BE HERE
FOR ME WHEN I'M HURT.
HE WILL MAKE MY
HURTS BETTER.

Because I suffer and am in need, let the Lord think of me. You are my help and the One Who sets me free. O my God, do not wait.

PSALM 40:17

[THE LORD SAID,] "IN THIS WORLD YOU WILL HAVE TROUBLE. BUT TAKE HEART! I HAVE OVERCOME THE WORLD."

JOHN 16:33 NIV

The little troubles we suffer now for a short time are making us ready for the great things God is going to give us forever.

2 CORINTHIANS 4:17

[Jesus said,] "Come to Me. . . .
I will give you rest."

MATTHEW 11:28

---

*We know that God makes all things work together
for the good of those who love Him and are
chosen to be a part of His plan.*

ROMANS 8:28

---

*Even if I walk into trouble, [God] will
keep my life safe.*

PSALM 138:7

GIVE ALL YOUR WORRIES TO [GOD] BECAUSE HE CARES FOR YOU.

1 PETER 5:7

I CALL TO GOD; GOD WILL HELP ME.

PSALM 55:17 MSG

"Those who have sorrow are happy,
because they will be comforted."

MATTHEW 5:4

Is anyone among you suffering?
He should pray.

JAMES 5:13

"You are sad now. I will see you again
and then your hearts will be full of joy.
No one can take your joy from you."

JOHN 16:22

God is our safe place.

PSALM 46:1

[God] gives us comfort in all our troubles.

2 CORINTHIANS 1:4

GIVE ALL YOUR CARES TO THE LORD AND HE WILL GIVE YOU STRENGTH.

PSALM 55:22

Our Lord Jesus Christ and God our Father loves us. Through His loving-favor He gives us comfort and hope that lasts forever.

2 THESSALONIANS 2:16

The Lord is good, a safe place in times
of trouble. And He knows those
who come to Him to be safe.

NAHUM 1:7

I am sure that our suffering now cannot be
compared to the shining-greatness that
[God] is going to give us.

ROMANS 8:18

WHEN HE FALLS, HE WILL NOT BE THROWN DOWN, BECAUSE THE LORD HOLDS HIS HAND.

PSALM 37:24

dear God,
thank you for coming to
my rescue when i'm hurt.
you always know just what i
need when i'm feeling down.
amen.

kindness

GOD WANTS ME TO BE
KIND TO OTHERS SO THEY
CAN SEE HIS LOVE IN ME.

DON'T EVER STOP BEING KIND. . . .
LET KINDNESS AND TRUTH
SHOW IN ALL YOU DO.

PROVERBS 3:3 ICB

"Give to any person who asks you for something.
If a person takes something from you,
do not ask for it back."

LUKE 6:30

Each of us should live to please his neighbor.
This will help him grow in faith.

ROMANS 15:2

*When someone does something bad to you,
do not do the same thing to him. When someone
talks about you, do not talk about him. Instead,
pray that good will come to him. You were
called to do this so you might receive
good things from God.*

1 PETER 3:9

---

*God has chosen you. You are holy and loved by
Him. Because of this, your new life should be full
of loving-pity. You should be kind to others
and have no pride. Be gentle and be
willing to wait for others.*

COLOSSIANS 3:12

"YOU MUST HAVE LOVING-KINDNESS JUST AS YOUR FATHER HAS LOVING-KINDNESS."

LUKE 6:36

The Lord. . .said, "Do what is right and be kind and show loving-pity to one another. . . . Do not make sinful plans in your hearts against one another."

ZECHARIAH 7:9–10

"LOVE YOUR ENEMIES! DO GOOD TO THEM. . . . THEN YOUR REWARD FROM HEAVEN WILL BE VERY GREAT, AND YOU WILL TRULY BE ACTING AS CHILDREN OF [GOD]."

LUKE 6:35 NLT

Laugh with your happy friends when they're happy; share tears when they're down.

ROMANS 12:15 MSG

We should do good to everyone. For sure, we should do good to those who belong to Christ.

GALATIANS 6:10

Be kind to Christian brothers and love them.

2 PETER 1:7

HE WHO HATES HIS NEIGHBOR SINS, BUT HAPPY IS HE WHO SHOWS LOVING-FAVOR TO THE POOR.

PROVERBS 14:21

---

*"Give to any person who asks you for something.
Do not say no to the man who wants
to use something of yours."*

MATTHEW 5:42

---

*Anyone who shows no loving-kindness will have no
loving-kindness shown to him when he is told he
is guilty. But if you show loving-kindness,
God will show loving-kindness to you
when you are told you are guilty.*

JAMES 2:13

Those who follow this way will have God's peace
and loving-kindness. They are the people of God.

GALATIANS 6:16

"The loving-kindness of the Lord
is given to the people of all
times who honor Him."

LUKE 1:50

"THOSE WHO SHOW LOVING-KINDNESS ARE HAPPY, BECAUSE THEY WILL HAVE LOVING-KINDNESS SHOWN TO THEM."

MATTHEW 5:7

dear God,
i want to be kind,
showing your love to
others every day!
amen.

loneliness

WHEN I FEEL ALONE,
I CAN TALK TO GOD.
HE'S ALWAYS HERE FOR ME.

"I am with you always."

"I am with you. No one will hurt you."

---

*"You will look for the Lord your God.
And you will find Him if you look for
Him with all your heart and soul."*

"WHEN YOU PASS THROUGH THE WATERS, I WILL BE WITH YOU."

"THE LORD KNOWS THOSE WHO ARE HIS."

2 Timothy 2:19

*The eyes of the LORD watch
over those who do right.*

1 Peter 3:12 NLT

*[The Lord said,] "See, I am with you.
I will care for you everywhere you go."*

Genesis 28:15

I will not be afraid of anything,
because You are with me.

PSALM 23:4

God has said, "I will never leave you
or let you be alone."

HEBREWS 13:5

"THEN YOU WILL CALL, AND THE LORD WILL
ANSWER. YOU WILL CRY, AND HE
WILL SAY, 'HERE I AM.'"

ISAIAH 58:9

*"The Lord is with you when you
are with Him. If you look for Him,
He will let you find Him."*

2 Chronicles 15:2

IF YOU LIVE IN LOVE, YOU LIVE BY THE HELP OF GOD AND GOD LIVES IN YOU.

1 John 4:16

"I will be a Father to you,
and you will be my sons and daughters,
says the Lord Almighty."

2 CORINTHIANS 6:18 NIV

[GOD SAID,] "I'VE CALLED
YOUR NAME. YOU'RE MINE."

ISAIAH 43:4 MSG

"[God] is not far from
each one of us."

ACTS 17:27

dear God,
i never need to feel alone.
you are always here to make
me feel safe and special.
you love me—your word
tells me so!
amen.

love

GOD'S LOVE FOR ME IS
SO BIG, I CAN'T EVEN
MEASURE IT.

IF GOD SO LOVED US, WE ALSO OUGHT TO LOVE ONE ANOTHER.

1 JOHN 4:11 NKJV

God has shown His love to us by sending His only Son into the world. God did this so we might have life through Christ.

1 JOHN 4:9

"No eye has ever seen or no ear has ever heard or no mind has ever thought of the wonderful things God has made ready for those who love Him."

1 CORINTHIANS 2:9

FOR I KNOW THAT NOTHING CAN KEEP US FROM THE LOVE OF GOD.

ROMANS 8:38

Love each other as Christian brothers.
Show respect for each other.

ROMANS 12:10

The love of God has come into our hearts through
the Holy Spirit Who was given to us.

ROMANS 5:5

The Lord takes care of all who love Him.

PSALM 145:20

GOD IS LOVE. IF YOU LIVE IN LOVE, YOU LIVE BY
THE HELP OF GOD AND GOD LIVES IN YOU.

1 JOHN 4:16

You obey [God] when you do this one thing,
"Love your neighbor as you love yourself."

GALATIANS 5:14

This is love! It is not that we loved God but that
He loved us. For God sent His Son to pay
for our sins with His own blood.

1 John 4:10

GOD HAS TAUGHT YOU TO LOVE EACH OTHER.

1 Thessalonians 4:9

"God so loved the world that
He gave His only Son."

John 3:16

God showed His love to us. While we were still
sinners, Christ died for us.

ROMANS 5:8

Dear friends, if God loved us that much,
then we should love each other.

1 JOHN 4:11

WE HAVE THESE THREE: FAITH AND HOPE AND LOVE, BUT THE GREATEST OF THESE IS LOVE.

1 CORINTHIANS 13:13

"This is what I tell you to do: Love each other just as I have loved you. No one can have greater love than to give his life for his friends."

JOHN 15:12–13

"You are to love each other. You must love each other as I have loved you. If you love each other, all men will know you are My followers."

JOHN 13:34–35

LOVE EACH OTHER WITH A KIND HEART AND WITH A MIND THAT HAS NO PRIDE.

1 PETER 3:8

The Lord came to us from far away, saying,
"I have loved you with a love that lasts forever.
So I have helped you come to Me
with loving-kindness."

JEREMIAH 31:3

"I HAVE LOVED YOU JUST AS MY FATHER HAS LOVED ME. STAY IN MY LOVE."

JOHN 15:9

" 'You must love the Lord your God with all your
heart and with all your soul and with all your
mind.' This is the first and greatest of the Laws.
The second is like it, 'You must love your
neighbor as you love yourself.' "

MATTHEW 22:37–39

dear God,
please help me
love others as much as
you love me!
amen.

obedience

OBEDIENCE IS A VERY BIG
WORD! IT MEANS TO DO
WHAT GOD'S WORD SAYS.
DOING WHAT GOD SAYS
SHOWS JUST HOW
MUCH I LOVE HIM.

We are taught to have nothing to do with
that which is against God. We are to have nothing
to do with the desires of this world. We are to
be wise and to be right with God. We are
to live God-like lives in this world.

<small>TITUS 2:12</small>

THOSE WHO OBEY WHAT THEY HAVE
BEEN TAUGHT ARE HAPPY.

<small>PROVERBS 29:18 ICB</small>

"Let your light shine in front of men. Then they will
see the good things you do and will honor
your Father Who is in heaven."

<small>MATTHEW 5:16</small>

*God is helping you obey Him. God is doing
what He wants done in you.*

PHILIPPIANS 2:13

---

*For if a man belongs to Christ, he is a new person.
The old life is gone. New life has begun.*

2 CORINTHIANS 5:17

"THE ONE WHO LOVES ME IS THE ONE WHO HAS MY TEACHING AND OBEYS IT."

JOHN 14:21

---

*Remember this, whatever good thing
you do, the Lord will pay you for it.*

EPHESIANS 6:8

SO GIVE YOURSELVES TO GOD. STAND AGAINST
THE DEVIL AND HE WILL RUN AWAY FROM YOU.

JAMES 4:7

---

*We will receive from Him whatever we ask if
we obey Him and do what He wants.*

1 JOHN 3:22

---

*Children. . .obey your parents.
This is the right thing to do.*

EPHESIANS 6:1

---

*We take hold of every thought
and make it obey Christ.*

2 CORINTHIANS 10:5

Do not. . .get tired of doing good. If we do
not give up, we will get what is coming
to us at the right time.

GALATIANS 6:9

You are being made more like Christ.
He is the One Who made you.

COLOSSIANS 3:10

THE MAN WHO OBEYS GOD AND DOES WHAT
HE WANTS DONE WILL LIVE FOREVER.

1 JOHN 2:17

Have your roots planted deep in Christ.
Grow in Him. Get your strength from Him.
Let Him make you strong in the faith
as you have been taught.

COLOSSIANS 2:7

CHILDREN, OBEY YOUR PARENTS IN EVERYTHING. THE LORD IS PLEASED WHEN YOU DO.

COLOSSIANS 3:20

Always do your work well for the Lord.
You know that whatever you do
for Him will not be wasted.

1 CORINTHIANS 15:58

dear God,
i want to obey
your word every day in
everything i do.
amen.

patience

I WILL BE PATIENT AND
TRUST GOD—ALWAYS
WAITING WITH A
HAPPY HEART.

PATIENCE AND ENCOURAGEMENT COME FROM GOD.

ROMANS 15:5 ICB

Rest in the Lord and be willing to wait for Him.

PSALM 37:7

You must be willing to wait without giving up.
After you have done what God wants you to
do, God will give you what He promised you.

HEBREWS 10:36

Do not let yourselves get tired of doing good.

GALATIANS 6:9

GOD'S PEOPLE NEED TO KEEP TRUE TO GOD'S WORD AND STAY FAITHFUL TO JESUS.

REVELATION 14:12

---

*Learn well how to wait so you will be strong
and complete and in need of nothing.*

JAMES 1:4

We are glad for our troubles also. We know that troubles help us learn not to give up. When we have learned not to give up, it shows we have stood the test. When we have stood the test, it gives us hope.

ROMANS 5:3–4

The God Who helps you not to give up and gives you strength will help you think so you can please each other as Christ Jesus did.

ROMANS 15:5

MAY THE LORD LEAD YOUR HEARTS INTO THE LOVE OF GOD. MAY HE HELP YOU AS YOU WAIT FOR CHRIST.

2 THESSALONIANS 3:5

BE WILLING TO WAIT FOR THE LORD TO COME
AGAIN. . . . BE STRONG IN YOUR HEARTS
BECAUSE THE LORD IS COMING AGAIN SOON.

James 5:7–8

Do not be lazy. Be like those who have faith
and have not given up. They will receive
what God has promised them.

Hebrews 6:12

Do not be quick in spirit to be angry.
For anger is in the heart of fools.

Ecclesiastes 7:9

For we belong to Christ if we keep on trusting
Him to the end just as we trusted Him at first.

HEBREWS 3:14

LET US HOLD ON TO THE HOPE WE SAY WE HAVE AND NOT BE CHANGED. WE CAN TRUST GOD THAT HE WILL DO WHAT HE PROMISED.

HEBREWS 10:23

Let us keep looking to Jesus. Our faith comes from
Him and He is the One Who makes it perfect. He did
not give up when He had to suffer shame and die on
a cross. He knew of the joy that would be His later.
Now He is sitting at the right side of God.

HEBREWS 12:2

But the fruit that comes from having the Holy Spirit in our lives is: love, joy, peace, not giving up, being kind, being good, having faith, being gentle, and being the boss over our own desires.

GALATIANS 5:22–23

GOD HAS CHOSEN YOU. YOU ARE HOLY AND LOVED BY HIM. BECAUSE OF THIS, YOUR NEW LIFE SHOULD BE FULL OF LOVING-PITY. YOU SHOULD BE KIND TO OTHERS AND HAVE NO PRIDE. BE GENTLE AND BE WILLING TO WAIT FOR OTHERS.

COLOSSIANS 3:12

Use the Word of God to help them do right.
You must be willing to wait for people to
understand what you teach as you teach them.

2 Timothy 4:2

A MAN WITH A BAD TEMPER STARTS FIGHTS, BUT HE WHO IS SLOW TO ANGER QUIETS FIGHTING.

Proverbs 15:18

It is good that one should be quiet and wait for the
saving power of the Lord.

Lamentations 3:26

dear God,
it's hard to be
patient. please help me
wait with a smile on
my face.
amen.

prayer

WHENEVER I PRAY,
GOD IS ALWAYS LISTENING.
HE NEVER GOES TO SLEEP!

LEARN TO PRAY ABOUT EVERYTHING.
GIVE THANKS TO GOD AS YOU ASK
HIM FOR WHAT YOU NEED.

PHILIPPIANS 4:6

---

*"Whatever you ask for when you pray, have faith
that you will receive it. Then you will get it."*

MARK 11:24

---

*GOD's there, listening for all who pray,
for all who pray and mean it.*

PSALM 145:18 MSG

[God said,] "When you call on me,
when you come and pray to me, I'll listen."

JEREMIAH 29:12 MSG

"IF YOU GET YOUR LIFE FROM ME AND MY WORDS LIVE IN YOU, ASK WHATEVER YOU WANT. IT WILL BE DONE FOR YOU."

JOHN 15:7

"When you pray, go into a room by yourself.
After you have shut the door, pray to your
Father Who is in secret. Then your Father
Who sees in secret will reward you."

MATTHEW 6:6

"ASK, AND WHAT YOU ARE ASKING
FOR WILL BE GIVEN TO YOU."

MATTHEW 7:7

---

*We are sure that if we ask anything that [God]
wants us to have, He will hear us. If we are
sure He hears us when we ask,
we can be sure He will give
us what we ask for.*

1 JOHN 5:14–15

---

*Pray for the things that are needed. You must
watch and keep on praying. Remember to
pray for all Christians.*

EPHESIANS 6:18

THE LORD LISTENS WHEN I PRAY TO HIM.

Psalm 4:3 icb

The prayer from the heart
of a man right with God
has much power.

James 5:16

We will receive from Him
whatever we ask if we obey
Him and do what He wants.

1 John 3:22

Let us give thanks all the time to
God through Jesus Christ.
Our gift to Him is to give thanks.

Hebrews 13:15

"Your Father knows what you
need before you ask Him."

MATTHEW 6:8

"Whatever you ask in My name, I will do it so the
shining-greatness of the Father may be
seen in the Son. Yes, if you ask
anything in My name, I will do it."

JOHN 14:13–14

"All things you ask for in prayer,
you will receive if you have faith."

MATTHEW 21:22

I ASK YOU TO PRAY MUCH FOR ALL MEN AND TO GIVE THANKS FOR THEM.

1 TIMOTHY 2:1

dear God,
i'm so glad that i can
talk to you. you always hear
my prayers. thank you for
loving me so much
amen.

sharing

GOD HAS GIVEN ME
SO MUCH. I CAN SHARE
WITH OTHERS!

[YOU] SHOULD GIVE MUCH TO THOSE IN NEED AND BE READY TO SHARE.

1 Timothy 6:18

"When you have a supper, ask poor people.
Ask those who cannot walk and those who are blind.
You will be happy if you do this. They cannot pay
you back. You will get your reward when the people
who are right with God are raised from the dead."

Luke 14:13–14

"If you have two coats, give one to him who has
none. If you have food, you must share some."

Luke 3:11

God can give you all you need. He will give you more than enough. You will have everything you need for yourselves. And you will have enough left over to give when there is a need.

2 CORINTHIANS 9:8

GOD LOVES A MAN WHO GIVES BECAUSE HE WANTS TO GIVE.

2 CORINTHIANS 9:7

"When you give, do not let your left hand know what your right hand gives. Your giving should be in secret. Then your Father Who sees in secret will reward you."

MATTHEW 6:3–4

*"If your brother becomes poor and is not able to
pay you what he owes, then you should help him
as you would help a stranger or visitor."*

LEVITICUS 25:35

---

*"Be free in giving to your brother, to those in
need, and to the poor in your land."*

DEUTERONOMY 15:11

---

*Happy is the man who cares for the poor.
The Lord will save him in times of trouble.*

PSALM 41:1

"EVERY MAN SHOULD GIVE AS HE IS ABLE, AS THE LORD YOUR GOD HAS GIVEN TO YOU."

DEUTERONOMY 16:17

"GIVE, AND IT WILL BE GIVEN TO YOU.
YOU WILL HAVE MORE THAN ENOUGH. . . .
THE WAY YOU GIVE TO OTHERS IS THE
WAY YOU WILL RECEIVE IN RETURN."

LUKE 6:38

He who shows kindness to a poor man gives
to the Lord and He will pay him in
return for his good act.

PROVERBS 19:17

We must remember what the Lord Jesus said,
"We are more happy when we give
than when we receive."

Acts 20:35

GOD WILL GIVE YOU ENOUGH SO YOU CAN ALWAYS GIVE TO OTHERS. THEN MANY WILL GIVE THANKS TO GOD FOR SENDING GIFTS THROUGH US.

2 Corinthians 9:11

dear God,
help me to remember that
everything i have is a gift
from you. help me share
these gifts with others.
amen.

thanks

I WILL START MY PRAYERS WITH A GREAT BIG "THANK YOU" TO GOD, BECAUSE HE IS SO GOOD TO ME.

*I will give thanks to the Lord
with all my heart. I will tell of all
the great things You have done.*

PSALM 9:1

---

*Always give thanks for all things
to God the Father in the name
of our Lord Jesus Christ.*

EPHESIANS 5:20

I WILL SPEAK WITH THE VOICE OF THANKS, AND TELL OF ALL YOUR GREAT WORKS.

PSALM 26:7

GIVE THANKS TO THE LORD, FOR HE IS GOOD!

PSALM 136:1 NKJV

"O give thanks to the Lord.
Call upon His name. Let the
people know what He has done."

1 CHRONICLES 16:8

In everything give thanks.
This is what God wants you
to do because of Christ Jesus.

1 THESSALONIANS 5:18

Do not be guilty of telling bad stories
and of foolish talk. These things are not for
you to do. Instead, you are to give
thanks for what God has done for you.

EPHESIANS 5:4

THANK GOD FOR HIS GREAT GIFT.

2 CORINTHIANS 9:15

Give thanks to God in the
meetings of worship.

PSALM 68:26

I will give thanks to the Lord
because He is right and good.
I will sing praise to the name
of the Lord Most High.

PSALM 7:17

I thank Christ Jesus our Lord
for the power and strength He
has given me. He trusted me
and gave me His work to do.

1 TIMOTHY 1:12

GIVE THANKS TO GOD AS YOU ASK HIM FOR WHAT YOU NEED.

PHILIPPIANS 4:6

**EVERYTHING GOD MADE IS GOOD.
WE SHOULD NOT PUT ANYTHING ASIDE IF WE
CAN TAKE IT AND THANK GOD FOR IT.**

1 TIMOTHY 4:4

---

*We give thanks to You, O God.
We give thanks that Your name
is near. Men tell about the
great things You have done.*

PSALM 75:1

---

*Jesus looked up and said, "Father,
I thank You for hearing Me."*

JOHN 11:41

I ALWAYS THANK GOD WHEN
I SPEAK OF YOU IN MY PRAYERS.

PHILEMON 1:4

Let us honor and thank the God and Father of
our Lord Jesus Christ. He has already given
us a taste of what heaven is like.

EPHESIANS 1:3

Your life should be full of thanks to [God].

COLOSSIANS 2:7

Let us thank the God and Father of our Lord Jesus Christ. It was through His loving-kindness that we were born again to a new life and have a hope that never dies. This hope is ours because Jesus was raised from the dead.

1 PETER 1:3

LET THE PEACE OF CHRIST HAVE POWER OVER YOUR HEARTS. YOU WERE CHOSEN AS A PART OF HIS BODY. ALWAYS BE THANKFUL.

COLOSSIANS 3:15

dear God,
thank you for all the
good things you give me.
i love you, God!
amen.

worry

EVEN WHEN I CAN'T BE IN CHARGE OF THINGS THAT HAPPEN, GOD DOESN'T WANT ME TO WORRY—HE WANTS ME TO LET HIM TAKE CARE OF EVERYTHING.

"I tell you this: Do not worry about your life.
Do not worry about what you are going to eat
and drink. Do not worry about what you are going
to wear. Is not life more important than food?
Is not the body more important than clothes?"

MATTHEW 6:25

**DO NOT WORRY. LEARN TO PRAY ABOUT
EVERYTHING. GIVE THANKS TO GOD AS
YOU ASK HIM FOR WHAT YOU NEED.**

PHILIPPIANS 4:6

"Which of you can make himself a little taller by
worrying? Why should you worry about clothes?
Think how the flowers grow. They do not work
or make cloth. But I tell you that Solomon
in all his greatness was not dressed as
well as one of these flowers."

MATTHEW 6:27–29

I KNOW THAT NOTHING CAN KEEP US FROM THE LOVE OF GOD.

ROMANS 8:38

God will give you everything you need because of His great riches in Christ Jesus.

PHILIPPIANS 4:19

"Do not worry about tomorrow. Tomorrow will have its own worries. The troubles we have in a day are enough for one day."

MATTHEW 6:34

You have turned my crying into dancing. . . .
So my soul may sing praise to You, and not be quiet.
O Lord my God, I will give thanks to You forever.

PSALM 30:11–12

THANKS BE TO THE LORD, WHO CARRIES OUR HEAVY LOADS DAY BY DAY. HE IS THE GOD WHO SAVES US.

PSALM 68:19

The peace of God is much greater than the human mind can understand. This peace will keep your hearts and minds through Christ Jesus.

PHILIPPIANS 4:7

*It is good to give thanks to the Lord, and sing
praises to Your name, O Most High. It is good to
tell of Your loving-kindness in the morning,
and of how faithful You are at night.*

Psalm 92:1–2

---

*God did not keep His own Son for Himself
but gave Him for us all. Then with His Son,
will He not give us all things?*

Romans 8:32

THERE IS NO WISDOM AND NO UNDERSTANDING AND NO WORDS THAT CAN STAND AGAINST THE LORD.

Proverbs 21:30

God is faithful. He will not allow you to be tempted more than you can take. But when you are tempted, He will make a way for you to keep from falling into sin.

1 Corinthians 10:13

"PEACE I LEAVE WITH YOU. MY PEACE I GIVE TO YOU. I DO NOT GIVE PEACE TO YOU AS THE WORLD GIVES. DO NOT LET YOUR HEARTS BE TROUBLED OR AFRAID."

John 14:27

If you follow Christ. . .God will be happy with you. Men will think well of you also. Work for the things that make peace and help each other become stronger Christians.

Romans 14:18–19

dear God,
thank you for taking
my worries away.

amen.